GRIEF

Is There More Than Moving On?

Nicholas Wolterstorff

ISBN: 0615867731
ISBN-13: 978-0615867731

ABOUT THIS SERIES

VeriTalks were created to cultivate ongoing conversations seeded by live Veritas Forum events.

Each VeriTalk includes both the original talk and audience Q&A to draw you more intimately into the conversation. Discussion questions—both personal and intellectual—are incorporated into the talk to deepen your engagement with the material, ideally in the company of friends. The questions are repeated at the end of the book for easy reference.

We hope this series will catalyze your exploration of True Life.

CONTENTS

ACKNOWLEDGMENTS

This talk was originally presented at The Veritas Forum at Mayo Clinic in 2011 under the title, "Living With Grief: Nicholas Wolterstorff Reflects on Grief and Love."

Many thanks to the students, faculty and campus organizations who helped create this event.

GRIEF: IS THERE MORE THAN MOVING ON?

For me, it's always good to be back in my home state of Minnesota. A quiet sort of beauty. Not big peaks that'll strike you in the face, but rolling hills and greenery, corn and soybeans. Thank you for the invitation to talk.

What Grief Is—And Is Not

Our son Eric was killed in a mountain climbing accident in Austria on June 11, 1983. What I have to say to you today consists of some of the reflections evoked in me by that painful event and by its aftermath in my own life.

You will find some of my reflections today – not all of them – in the little book I wrote, *Lament for a Son*. It's a book in which there's a great deal of silence, white space, empty pages. I think that in the face of death we should not chatter.

Let me begin with a few reflections on what grief is. When

GRIEF

I wrote *Lament for a Son*, I neither understood much about grief, nor did I want to take much time and energy to understand it. The book is not about grief; it's a cry of grief. Those are two different things.

In the book I said that grief presupposes love; if I had not loved Eric, his death would not have plunged me into grief. But that's pretty much all I understood about grief at the time, that grief presupposes love. I think I can now say more about what it consists of than I could then.

To find where grief is located in our human existence, maybe it helps to mention, first, some of the places where it is not located.

Valorization structure. We human beings are so created that we find certain subjective experiences pleasant; other subjective experiences unpleasant or distasteful; and a fair number of subjective experiences neutral, neither here nor there. Most of us like the taste of chocolate ice cream. Conversely, I've never yet come across somebody who likes the smell of sulfur. In short, our experiences are valorized; they have experiential value for us, positive or negative. One might call this structure of the human self – to give it a fancy philosopher's term – the *valorization* structure.

Grief is not located within the workings of the valorization structure. My grief over Eric's death is not to be put in the same bag as my dislike of the smell of sulfur; the two are very different.

Pain. Pain is a dimension of the human self different from the valorization structure. Pain is a physiological phenomenon. Correction: though most pain has a physiological basis, not all of it does. Though distinct from the valorization structure, pain does fall within the valorization structure in that most of us, most of the time, don't like pain.

It was not by virtue of the workings of my physiological structure that I was cast into grief by Eric's death. As I said before, to locate grief we have to look at the place of love within the human self. But love comes in different forms. So what form of love yields grief?

Benevolence? One form of love is benevolence. Benevolence is willing and working to advance someone's good. Benevolence is not the form of love relevant to grief. Attempts at benevolence sometimes fail; when they do, what we feel is not grief but regret, frustration, disappointment, that sort of thing.

Attraction? A second form of love is love as attraction. This sort of love is at work when you are drawn to something for its worth. It's love as attraction that one is referring to when one says, "I just love the late Beethoven string quartets." One is drawn to them on account of their worth. You can all easily provide other examples of the same thing.

When the object of one's attraction-love changes, so that it's no longer admirable and attractive, or when it becomes inaccessible, or decays, dies or goes out of existence, one feels regret and disappointment, not grief. If I could no longer listen to the late Beethoven string quartets, it would be odd to say that I'm grieving over this. I would instead be deeply regretful.

Attachment? A third form of love is love as attachment, the love that consists of being attached to somebody or something. Somehow or other one became attached to this person, this animal, this object. Love as attachment is strange. It's not like love as attraction. You can get attached to something without thinking it's particularly admirable or attractive. Some cat shows up on your doorstep one winter day, you take it in, you become very attached to it; but you don't think it's the finest cat around. Your neighbor's cat is better, no doubt about it. Yours may not win finest-of-the-show in a cat show; but you are attached to it.

Attachment—this will become important later—attachment gives rise to desires and endeavors. It's not to be identified with those; rather, it gives rise to desires and endeavors with respect to the thing or person to which you are attached.

Some of those desires may be desires for benefits to the lover; we like having our children around. But a lot of them are desires not with respect to one's own well-being but with respect to the well-being of the one loved. You want your your child's welfare; you want your child to flourish. What happens as the result of our attachment to our children is that we rejoice with them over their attainments, not just our own; and we sorrow with them over their failures, not just our own; over their disappointments, their frustrations, their broken bones. This is how love as attachment works.

I suggest that to locate grief we have to look for love as attachment. That's where it's located. Grief occurs, so I suggest, when the object of one's attachment dies, disappears, or is destroyed, or when its well-being is significantly impaired or diminished and there's no hope of that changing.

Wanting the impossible. More specifically, grief is wanting the loved one back, wanting the undoing of his or her destruction or impairment, while at the same time knowing that that's impossible. Let me say it again: grief occurs when that to which one is attached has been destroyed or impaired and there is no hope of that being undone.

Grief is wanting it to be undone while at the same time knowing, or firmly believing, that it cannot be undone; the more intense the wanting it to be undone, the more intense the grief.

Wanting intensely the continued earthly life of my son, to whom I was attached, when I knew that could not be; that was my grief. I am also thinking here of the woman who, when I was talking about these matters, came up to me afterwards and said, surreptitiously, so that nobody could overhear her, that her grief was not over the fact that her son had died but over the fact that he could never be what she had always hoped and expected he would be; then, before I could ask her to explain, she moved away.

Grief is *wanting* the destruction or impairment to be undone, not just wishing it to be undone. I remember that when I was a teenager out on the prairies of southwest Minnesota I wished to become a major league baseball pitcher, wished to become one of the very best, a 20-game winner. I fantasized about it. But the fact that my wish has not been realized has caused me no grief whatsoever; the reason it hasn't is that it was not something that I really wanted. Being lousy at baseball, I took no steps whatsoever in the direction of becoming a baseball pitcher. I wished, but did not want.

Grief requires wanting, not just wishing. And you have to believe that what you want is impossible. Otherwise what you have is not grief but hope. Maybe hope against hope, maybe worried, anxious hope; but still hope. To say it once again: grief occurs when you are attached to someone or something and that someone or something dies, or changes, or disappears; grief is wanting with all your heart what you know or believe is impossible.

QUESTIONS FOR DISCUSSION

Professor Wolterstorff suggests that to locate grief we have to look at love as attachment. Does your experience of grief fit with this understanding of love?

GRIEF

Tears and agitation are, of course, typical expressions of grief, but they're not the thing itself; they're not even necessary. A person can grieve quietly. It's important for friends and counselors to keep this in mind. Because there are no tears does not mean that there is no grief.

Immobilizing. In grief, wanting collides with knowing. I desperately wanted Eric to be alive; but I knew that he was dead and could not be brought back to life. Grief is banging your head against the wall. It's the frustration of wanting what you know can't be.

That's what accounts for something that probably all of you have noticed, namely, the immobility of the person in grief. If you're frightened, you can run away or hide. If you're angry, you can avenge yourself.   But when you're in grief, there's nothing you can do, short of trying to change yourself.

Irrational. Given that grief is wanting what you know can't be, grief is, in a way, irrational; it makes no sense to want what you know can't be. In this way too, grief is different from fear and anger. Some fear is irrational, and some anger is irrational; but they aren't as such irrational. It often makes perfectly good sense to be fearful or angry. Grief, by contrast, is inherently irrational.

It's that irrationality at the heart of grief that makes people who are not personally acquainted with grief want to say to the person in grief, "Get over it. Shape up. No use crying over spilled milk. You can't bring them back." It's also that irrationality, that banging your head against the wall, that makes many people in our culture regard the person in grief as in need of therapy or counseling.

I grant that some grieving people do need therapy; their

6

grief is pathological. But let me say as emphatically as I can that though there is something irrational about grief, grief is not as such pathological. If you loved your child, then you just will feel grief upon learning of his or her death. That's not pathology. That's things working the way they should work.

Admirable. Now let me add that if your love was an admirable thing in your life, then your grief is also an admirable thing in your life. If your child was worth loving when alive, then your child is worth grieving over when dead. Grief is existential no-saying to the loss of the loved one. Grief is existential tribute to the worth of the one loved and to the worth of the love.

Attachment-based. Let me make one more point about the nature of grief. I observed earlier that our attachments give rise to various commitments and desires with respect to the one loved. Those change over the years. The attachment you have to your child when an infant gives rise to desires and commitments that are quite different from those you experience when your child is a teenager. Or they should. There's something sick if they don't grow along with the child.

But when the object of the attachment doesn't grow and mature but is destroyed or seriously impaired, that whole complex of desires and commitments is deprived of its object. The picture I get in my mind is the picture of all those desires and commitments that I and my wife, friends, and others had with respect to Eric now floating loose. There's nothing that they're attached to anymore; that's a big part of why grief is so devastating.

Desires, commitments, and so forth are a huge part of the self in all of us. Grief is accompanied by the destruction of that part of the self. All those desires and commitments are now floating free, loose, unattached. In my book *Lament* I put it like this: "The person in grief has to learn to live around the hole in himself that the loss of the loved one created."

QUESTIONS FOR DISCUSSION

Do you agree with Professor Wolterstorff's characterization of grief as irrational but not pathological, admirable but devastating?

Have you experienced the "floating loose" of your desires, when the object of your attachment is destroyed? How did (or do) you respond?

? For audience questions related to this topic, see page 21 (*Does grief have an endpoint?*) and page 22 (*Why is consolation often met with disdain?*).

LIVING WITH GRIEF: OWNING OR DISOWNING

That was about the nature of grief; now a few comments about living with grief. I will then conclude with some suggestions for what to say to the person in grief.

It appears to me that the most common view in contemporary western society on how to live with grief is that we should all work towards disowning our grief. Let me explain what I mean.

Narrative identity. I'm retired now; but back in the days when I still taught, when a new student came into my office I would often open the discussion by putting to them a completely open-ended question, namely, "Tell me who you are."

In response to that open-ended question some students would mention interests of theirs or character traits that they thought I might be interested in; but almost always what they also did is tell me a narrative, a story, about events in their life that they thought would be important for me to know and that they themselves thought to be important.

Each of them had what one might call a "narrative identity"; and they presented a bit of that to me as an answer to my question, "Tell me who you are."

So when I say that someone owns their grief, I mean that it's part of their narrative identify, part of the story about themselves that they give in answer to the question, "Tell me who you are." When someone says, "Tell me who you are," the person who owns their grief says something like, "I am one who suffered the grief of losing a son. You should know that that's part of who I am."

It may not be the first thing that she mentions; depending on the situation, she may not mention it at all. But in lots of situations her grief is part of the story she tells about herself. It belongs to her narrative identity.

Conversely, to disown one's grief is to bring oneself to the point where, in relating one's narrative identity, one never mentions the loss, either because one has forgotten it or because one doesn't think it's very important. "But I think I remember hearing that you lost a six-year-old son." "Oh, yes, I did, now that you mention it. I forgot about that." That's a case of disowning the loss.

Disowning grief. Back to the point: it appears to me that the most common view in contemporary western society as to how to live with grief is that one should work towards disowning it. Take note of our language: putting it behind you, getting over it, getting on with things, getting on with life, no use crying over spilled milk. Such language is the language of disowning. So far as I can tell – I might be wrong about this – disowning grief is also the idea underlying most of the books on stages of grief, on the grief process, on processing grief, and so forth. The goal, as far as I can tell, is eventually to get over your grief, to make it no longer part of who you are, to delete it eventually from your narrative identity. That's our modern way of dealing with grief.

A way of dealing with grief that was common in the ancient world was pretty much the opposite of our modern way. I have in mind the strategy recommended by the ancient Stoics, a dominant school of ethics in late antiquity. In place of our modern practice of dealing with grief after it occurs by trying to disown it, the Stoics recommended that we change ourselves so that grief hardly ever occurs.

How do we do that? By getting rid of, or preventing, attachments. Pull in your horns. Don't attach yourself to your children, to your cat, to your dog, to your house. That way, you won't feel grief when they die or are destroyed. That was the

Stoic recommendation. When one of the ancient Stoics was asked why he wasn't grieving over the death of his child, he is recorded as making the steely response, "But I always knew he would die someday."

Though there aren't many Stoics around anymore, stoicism did have a profound influence on western thought, including western Christianity. It powerfully influenced Saint Augustine's attitude in his early writings toward the death of his schoolmate and toward the death of his mother. He grieved in both cases; but after his conversion to Christianity from paganism he felt guilty for having grieved. So in his *Confessions* he confesses to God the sin of having loved his friend and his mother too much, his grief being the sign of having loved them too much. That is Christianized stoicism.

By the end of his life Augustine had changed his view. He then wrote that it was appropriate to grieve over the death of parents and friends. The crucial element in his change of mind was that whereas early in his Christian life he had viewed it as sinful to love someone in such a way that one grieves over his or her death, he eventually came to the view that such love was part of our created nature, not part of our sinful nature.

Owning grief. My own view is different from both the modern view and the ancient Stoic view. I do not accept the Stoic proposal that we should try to forestall grief by rooting out all our attachments; but neither do I think that we should allow the attachments to be formed and then try to disown the grief once it occurs. I think we should allow the attachments to develop and then own the grief that may ensue.

Here's my reason. It was a good thing about me that I loved my son, that I was attached to him, that I felt affection for him. That was not a bad thing about me, as the Stoics would insist, but a good thing. If I had not been attached to him, that would have been a bad thing. But given my attachment, his death inevitably cast me into grief. So why would that grief be a bad thing, something that I should try to root out, if my attachment was a good thing and the grief comes along with it? If my attachment was a good thing, why would my grief be a bad thing?

My view is that failure on my part to grieve would have been a bad thing. If it's a good thing to grieve over the death of a child, a parent, a friend, a pet — and I hold that it is — then we must own our grief, make it part of who we are, part of our narrative identity. Or maybe not *make* it part of our narrative identity but just allow it to become part.

And beyond owning our grief, I think we should each struggle toward eventually owning it redemptively, that is, owning it in such a way that some good comes out of it. What that good may be will differ profoundly from person to person; and whatever it proves to be, it may take one a long time to be able to own one's grief redemptively. Nobody ever does it immediately; and some, try though they may, never succeed in bringing it off. But that should be one's aim and hope.

QUESTIONS FOR DISCUSSION

How do you approach living with grief? Do you try to move on, avoid attachments, or something else?

Do you know anyone who has owned her grief and made it part of her narrative identity? What does it look like?

In response to a question from the audience (see page 27), Professor Wolterstorff suggested that by owning your grief, "Death shall not have the last word." What could it look like for you to own your own grief? Do you believe death has the last word?

In response to a question from the audience about what helps bring resilience in grief (see page 23), Professor Wolterstorff answered: "In my case, religious faith and hope, though my grief altered those. They don't stay the same either." How has your experience of grief altered your religious faith?

? For more audience questions related to this topic, see page 24 (*How do you explain that Saint Augustine thought that grief is a sin?*) and page 26 (*Do you believe in setting aside time for grieving?*).

GRIEF

WHAT TO SAY—AND NOT TO SAY

Let me close with some suggestions as to what you as friend, counselor, pastor or medical care person should say and not say to the grieving person. You will recognize that what I say here is in good measure based on my experience of what people said to me or did not say to me.

1. Say something. Worst of all is the friend who says nothing, absolutely nothing. Nothing is so excruciatingly painful as that. I now know why some people say nothing. They don't know what to say. They think they should say something wise, something helpful, something that's not a cliché; but they can't think of anything like that, so they say nothing. If you can't think of anything to say, just say that you can't think of anything to say but that you want me to know that you are with me in my grief. That's good enough.

2. Express your love for the grieving person. Express your love in words, if you can, but if you can't find the words to express it, express it in some other way – with a hug or whatever.

3. Do not downplay the grief. Do not say that really, it's not so bad, that the grieving person still has – I'm quoting – that the grieving person still has other children. Do not offer consolations of that sort. You're dealing with a broken, shattered human being. His or her way of inhabiting the world has been broken, crushed. That's bad, really bad. So don't say that it's not.

4. Do more listening than talking. Or if the grieving person doesn't want to talk, just be there, for her and with her. Be like Job's friends. Sit beside her on the mourning bench.

5. Sometimes you may have to help identify the grief. Help to name it. Sometimes grief – not for a person, but for things – is obscure. Helping to name it may be a difficult, delicate, even traumatic thing to do. I am thinking here of the person who came up to me after I gave a talk on grief and said that he was cast into grief by the wreckage of his car and that it took him half a year to identify what was really going on.

6. Offer correction gently. You may eventually conclude that the grief was misplaced, that the thing loved was not worth that much love or that the loss is not irrevocable. You may even conclude that the grief has become pathological. Offer corrections eventually, not immediately, and gently, not in a chastising tone but in the context of a listening love.

7. Praise. If the love was not misplaced, join in honoring and praising the person or thing loved. I can witness to you that such praise is painful but at the same time mysteriously healing. I think it is healing because it affirms the legitimacy of the grief.

8. Rephrase the "why?" Some people in grief will be asking why this happened, or why this happened to them. Almost always the one who asks this question will be thinking that God caused this death, and they want to know why God did that to them.

My own theology leads me to say that one should suggest that the question be rephrased. Something has gone amiss, awry, in God's world – this is my view. The early death of children is not part of how God meant things to go. Of course, that raises the question: Why have things gone amiss and awry in God's world in the way they have? To this question, we do not know the answer.

I am a professional philosopher and a semi-professional theologian. I think I am acquainted with all the theodicies that have been proposed over the past 2,500 years, all the attempts to explain the presence of evil in a God-created and God-sustained universe. To my mind, none of them is successful. We have to learn to live the unanswered question. Christians and other theists will not live the unanswered question without hope; but their hope is not an answer to the question.

9. Grief isolates. It is enormously important to realize and keep in mind that grief isolates. Grief does not unite, in spite of the old aphorism "there is company in misery." Grief isolates. It isolates for various reasons, one of them being that people go through grief in different paces and phases, and they find it alienating that their spouse, their siblings, whatever, are not going through it at the same pace and in the same phases.

10. Keep in mind that each person's grief has its own pace. And that there is no right or wrong pace. I have had people come up to me and say, "Is it right for me still to be grieving in the way that I am?" I have invariably said, "Of course." It is particularly important to remind members of the family that there is no right or wrong pace. I realize that there are stages in grief; but there is no right or wrong path, and no right or wrong pace, through those stages.

11. Don't say that you know what it's like. Don't say you know what it's like because you don't, and the grieving person knows that you don't. Each of us has, at most, a glimpse of what it's like. Grief is extremely particular. I think it's more particular than anything else in our human existence. There are similarities, indeed; but grief resists generalization.

QUESTIONS FOR DISCUSSION

What have you found to be particularly helpful or unhelpful in your own experience of grief?

Professor Wolterstorff says that "Something has gone amiss, awry, in God's world…Of course, that raises the question why have things gone amiss and awry in God's world…We have to learn to live with the unanswered question." Do you feel God is to blame for suffering and loss? Do you find the question of why tragedy happens to be unanswerable? Can you live with hope even with an unanswered question?

If you have a friend, relative or patient in the midst of grieving, could you apply any of Professor Wolterstorff's suggestions?

How do Professor Wolterstorff's reflections free you to grieve or to comfort a grieving friend, relative or patient?

QUESTION AND ANSWER

GRIEF

Summary of Questions from the Audience

- Does grief have an endpoint? (Answer on page 21)

- Why is consolation often met with disdain? (Answer on page 22)

- What do you think contributes to the resilience of people who have grieved through many thing in their life and thus have many holes that they have to work around? (Answer on page 23)

- How do you explain that Saint Augustine thought that grief is sin, when Jesus himself grieved over Lazarus? (Answer on page 24)

- Do you believe in setting aside time for grieving? (Answer on page 26)

- What does it look like for someone to own her grief redemptively? (Answer on page 27)

Question and Answer Session

Audience member: Does grief have an endpoint?

Wolterstorff: For some people, it does; but my view is that it should not have an endpoint. It does, however, change over time. Let me speak personally. I used to get lots of letters about my book, *Lament.* I answered all those letters with the exception of a few that I got early on from the members of a religious group who chastised me for my theology; it turned out that their monthly periodical had run a review of the book in which my theology was criticized. I remember as of yesterday sitting down at my desk to respond to these letters and finding that I was incapable of doing so; I was paralyzed. I could not argue theology in the face of Eric's death. Those are the only letters I have not answered.

Nowadays the communications almost all come by e-mail; and over and over the question is posed, "Does grief change over time? And does it end?"

Grief does change over time. I think that's mainly because you learn to live around the hole in your life, the gap. As you learn to live around it, it becomes less of a preoccupation. But every now and then some strange and unexpected chain of associations brings it all back; some experience makes you think of something, that makes you think of something else, that makes you think of a third thing, and soon the death of the one you loved is once again right there in front of you. That makes you feel the grief all over again. That's how it should be, in my view.

GRIEF

Audience member: Based on my observation, it seems that when you're consoling somebody with grief, the comment of, "I'll pray for you. I'll keep you in my prayers," is often met with some degree of disdain. Why would that be?

Wolterstorff: Maybe consolation takes different forms. But often it takes the form of saying to the grieving person, "Look, there are compensating things in your life; focus on those." I and my wife had five children. Some people said, "You still have your other children." I heard the implicit message as being, "You still have four children; so you shouldn't grieve over the loss of one." I bridle at that. Children are not like marbles. If you have five marbles and you lose one, you can go to Hobby Lobby and get a replacement. Children are not replaceable.

A consolation that religious people often offer is, "He's better off now because he's in heaven." But he's not here; that's the source of my grief. Your telling me that he is better off now because he is in heaven doesn't bring him back.

My experience has been that consolations are off target. Consolations try to distract the grieving person. I don't think the grieving person should be distracted. The grief is a good thing, not a bad thing; so don't try to distract him.

Audience member: What do you think contributes to the resilience of people who have grieved through many things and thus have many holes that they have to work around?

Wolterstorff: Friends of the right sort help. In my case, religious faith and hope helped. My grief altered those, however. They didn't stay the same; they got altered. One becomes more wary. But the answer is that some people are more fragile than others, less flexible. I'm walking around your question. I don't know the answer.

GRIEF

Audience member: How do you explain that Saint Augustine thought that grief is sin, when Jesus himself grieved over Lazarus?

Wolterstorff: When there are passages that we don't much like in certain texts, including passages that we don't much like in Scripture, so often they don't sink in; they make no impression. Late in his life Augustine noted that passage about Jesus' grief; earlier he had looked right past it.

A good deal of what accounted for that was that he was profoundly shaped in the first part of his career by Neoplatonism and Stoicism; that led him to think along the following lines: What counts about a human being is their soul, not their body. But their soul hasn't died, so why are you grieving? One should not be so attached to a flesh-and-blood human being as to grieve over their physical death.

You will find this line of thought explicitly stated in a little book *Of True Religion* that Augustine published at the same time as his *Confessions.* Think through your love for somebody and be sure it's got nothing to do with the person's body, only with the person's soul. That's straight Plato. It was the influence of Plato, coupled with the influence of Stoicism, that led him to look past things in Scripture.

Late in his life Augustine wrote *The City of God.* By then the influence of Platonism and Stoicism had weakened; and he now takes note of passages in Scripture that he had previously overlooked. He now employs Scripture to support his view that grief belongs to our created nature, not to our fallen nature.

Earlier Augustine said we should grieve with those who are grieving over the state of someone's soul because that soul's not religiously or morally healthy. Late in his life, he says we should grieve over bodily tribulations like death, starvation. A sea-change occurred in his thought; and in that change you have sort of a capsule of the history of the West with respect to grief.

GRIEF

Audience member: Do you believe in setting aside time for grieving? Or do you think that grieving is a natural thing? Should it happen when it happens? Should you let it happen when it feels like it's going to happen? Do you know what I mean?

Wolterstorff: If at all possible, don't put it away for now. If at all possible, don't put it away ever. Eric died in June; I'm a college professor, so I didn't have to teach at the time. I have no idea what I would have done if I had had to teach. I have no idea, because I was immobilized and couldn't understand why everybody else wasn't immobilized as well. I went to shop for groceries. The sight of people casually putting loaves of bread in their shopping carts made me wince. How can you do that so casually? Don't you know that the whole world is different now?

My wife and I have a friend, John, whose 21-year-old son died from cancer and whose wife died about four years later, also from cancer. John is an attorney. He took no time off after either of those deaths. It's not that he didn't love them. He took no time off. When my wife and I had dinner with him about a year after his wife died, it struck us both that he looked ravaged. He had not given himself time to grieve. He had stuffed it down, or tried to stuff it down. I think that's both a moral mistake and a psychological mistake.

Audience member: You talked about owning our grief and making it a part of or our narrative; and you said that we should try to own it redemptively. What do you mean by that? How does a person who owns her grief redemptively look different from a person who does not do that?

Wolterstorff: What I mean by trying to own one's grief redemptively is this: The grieving person is now a profoundly altered human being. I think they should try to bring themselves to a point where a good of some sort emerges from that profound change.

In my case, I wrote *Lament for a Son* and have given talks like the one I am giving now. That is something good that has come out of my loss. Other people will do something quite different. People have described to me the change that eventually emerged in their lives. They found themselves loving their remaining children in a different and better way. They found themselves perceiving the world more vividly and more gratefully than they did before. They became active in Compassionate Friends.

The goal is that this tragedy shall not be nothing but tragedy. Some people have been on the verge of saying to me, without ever actually saying, "Your book is a good thing. Maybe it made Eric's death" – and then they catch themselves. You see how the sentence finishes, right? They see that they shouldn't finish it; but they want to say something in the region. Some good emerged from my grief.

You, the grieving person, are altered. You see the world differently, you love people differently, your sense of what's important is different. Some good has emerged; death does not have the last word.

The best I can do is to say that you own your grief and own it redemptively. You own it in such a way that you say, "I'm better because of it." No way would I exchange my betterness for my son's death; that's what those people were on the verge of saying when they caught themselves. But I am better in some ways.

QUESTIONS FOR DISCUSSION

GRIEF

From *What Grief Is—And Is Not* **(page 5)**

- Professor Wolterstorff suggests that to locate grief, we have to look at love as attachment. Does your experience of grief fit with this understanding of love?

From *Nature of Grief* **(page 8)**

- Do you agree with Professor Wolterstorff's characterization of grief as irrational but not pathological, admirable but devastating?

- Have you experienced the "floating loose" of your desires, when the object of your attachment is destroyed? How did (or do) you respond?

From *Living with Grief: Owning or Disowning* **(page 13)**

- How do you approach living with grief? Do you try to move on, avoid attachments, or something else?

- Do you know anyone who has owned her grief and made it part of her narrative identity? What does it look like?

- What could it look like for you to own your own grief?

- In response to a question from the audience (see page 27), Professor Wolterstorff suggested that by owning your grief, "Death shall not have the last word." What could it look like for you to own your own grief? Do you believe death has the last word?

- In response to a question from the audience—What do you think contributes to the resilience of people who have grieved through many things? (see page 23)—Professor Wolterstorff answered: "In my case, religious faith and hope, though my grief altered those. They don't stay the same either." How has your experience of grief altered your religious faith?

From *What To Say—And Not To Say* **(page 17)**

- What have you found to be particularly helpful or unhelpful in your own experience of grief?

- Professor Wolterstorff says that "Something has gone amiss, awry, in God's world...Of course, that raises the question why have things gone amiss and awry in God's world...We have to learn to live with the unanswered question." Do you feel God is to blame for suffering and loss? Do you find the question of why tragedy happens to be unanswerable? Can you live with hope even with an unanswered question?

- If you have a friend, relative or patient in the midst of grieving, could you apply any of Professor Wolterstorff's suggestions?

- How do Professor Wolterstorff's reflections free you to grieve or to comfort a grieving friend, relative or patient?

ABOUT THE VERITAS FORUM

The Veritas Forum hosts university events that engage students and faculty in discussions about life's hardest questions and the relevance of Jesus Christ to all of life.

Every year, hundreds of university community members host, plan and coordinate a Veritas Forum on their local campuses, with guidance from national and regional staff across North America and Europe.

We seek to inspire the shapers of tomorrow's culture to connect their hardest questions with the person and story of Jesus Christ.

For more information about The Veritas Forum, including recordings and upcoming events, visit www.veritas.org.

4267851R00026

Made in the USA
San Bernardino, CA
09 September 2013